The Bruised Apple

Written and Illustrated by
Sarah Elizabeth

The Bruised Apple

ISBN: 979-8-9854728-0-6 (paperback)
ISBN: 979-8-9854728-1-3 (hardback)

Published by Sarah Elizabeth
sarah.elizabeth@twinklingsofhope.com

Attributions and permissions are located on page 39.

To You.

We pick up this bruised apple's story

as it got set in a market's bin

with other apples, shiny and red,

ready and waiting to be eaten.

A person passing by picked it up,

but, on seeing our apple's big bruise,

she swiftly set it down, for she thought,

What a bruise! Surely one I refuse.

The next who thought, ***I want that apple,*** saw the same bruise and put it back too, purposely placing it with its bruise facing up. Now passersby cried, "Eww!"

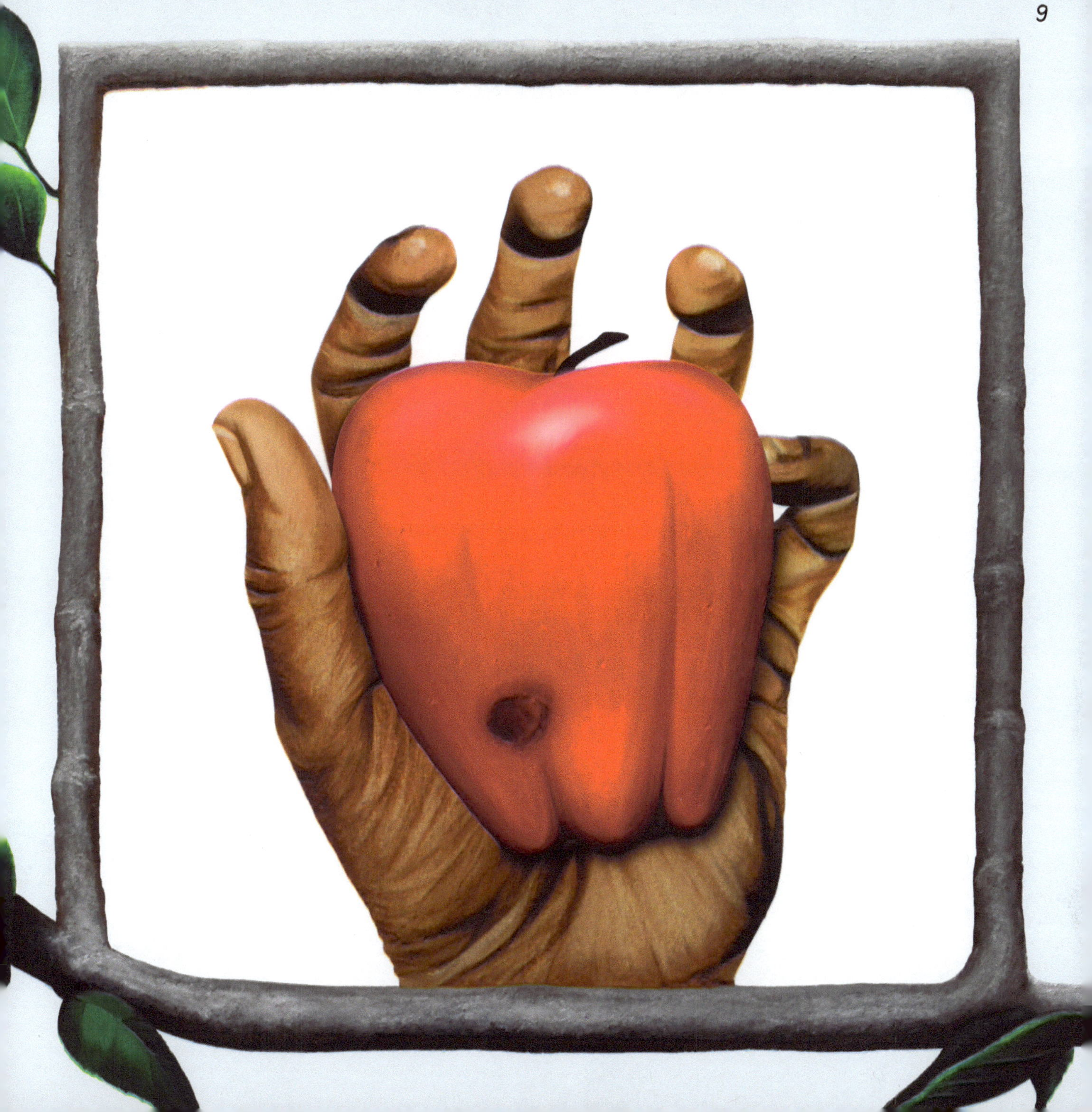

So each person chose other apples,
and when they were pulled out from below,
our apple would fall—tumbling, rolling,
and forming small spots that'd also show.

Once, it even bounced out of the bin
and plunged helplessly down to more hurt.
But, before hitting the ground, it rolled
off a leg and just picked up some dirt.

As it rolled, a kind soul lifted it

up, out of its set journey away,

and gently set it back in the bin,

where it waited the rest of that day.

When night set in, just a few were left.

Each bore bruises and some sported spots,

but the reasons they'd been rejected

did not stop their rescue; all got boxed!

In with the apples, there also went
broccoli, berries, and veggie roots;
all ready, now, to get shipped out with
a special purpose for this produce!

Off, they were carried, to a food bank,

where our apple was held briefly by

someone putting care into practice

to keep safe food the hungry's supply.

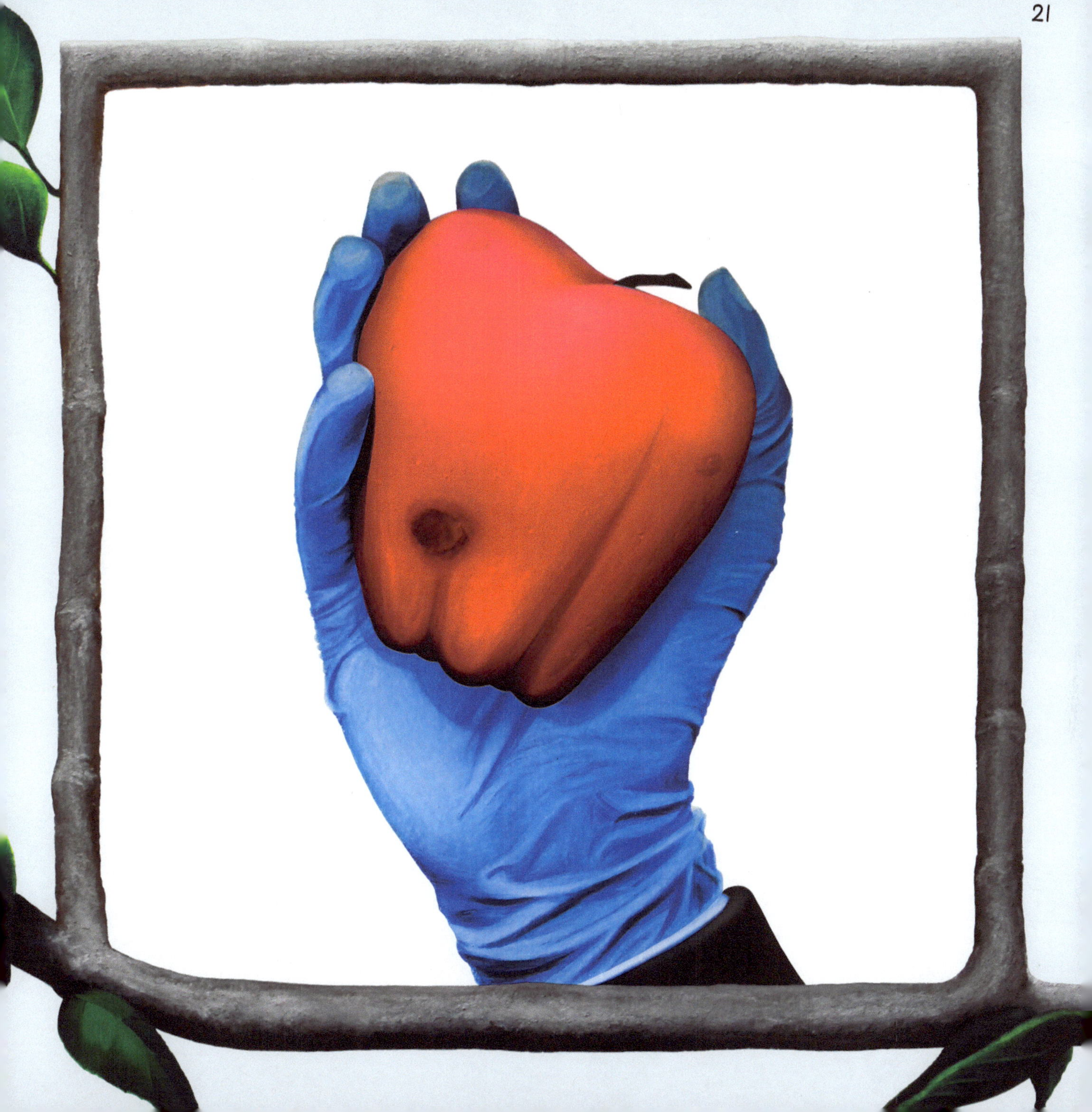

Now another box held our apple.

With it, a load of food was amassed

as boxes were sorted, packed, and stacked.

Their time to be delivered came fast!

They were sent to a food pantry, where,

by the helping hand of another,

our newly shined apple was put out

and was soon picked up by a mother.

She set the apple in a basket

with other food that would meet some needs

felt by her small, hungry family

anew every day as on life speeds.

Later that day, she washed their apple,

then ate its red peel and cut the rest.

When she gave it to her boy, he said,

"Thanks, Mom! Have I told you, you're the best?!"

He caught a glimpse of her smile starting
but setting his focus on his feast
let him imagine that her smile reached
her eyes, which the weight of worry creased.

"I'm sorry, God", *she prayed,* "I'm trying."
By faith, His Word reassured, My child,
keep trusting me through this hard trial;
my grace will keep all the reconciled.

Then a genuine smile lit her face
when her boy, with each and every bite,
would "Mmm" over the crunch and do a
silly wiggle to show his delight.

This apple was so juicy and sweet!

He was grateful it was his to eat.

the end

of

The Bruised Apple

Attributions

Cover Hand and Page 9:

Maño by Inko 6 is a photograph licensed under CC BY 4.0 https://creativecommons.org/licenses/by/4.0/legalcode. Drawn with chalk; oil pastel apple added in the edited illustration on page nine. Inko 6 has not endorsed this work.

Page 23:

U.S. Army National Guard photo by Captain Brendan Mackie is in the public domain under Creative Commons' CC-PD Mark 1.0. Chalk drawing of the hand; box and apple added. The National Guard has not endorsed this work.

Page 25:

U.S. Army National Guard photograph by Major Charles W. Westrip is licensed under Creative Commons' CC BY 4.0. https://creativecommons.org/licenses/by/4.0/legalcode. Pencil drawing of front left hand; sleeve altered, pastel apple added. The National Guard has not endorsed this work; I was drawn to the photos of their pandemic service.

Pages 7, 15, 35, and 37:

Photographs found on Pixabay. Each have the license: https://pixabay.com/service/terms/#license. Hands drawn in chalk; oil pastel apple, plate and pencil apple slices added. These photographers have not endorsed this work.

Pages 5, 17, 19, 21, and 39:

Emily Capellari gave me her hands as references for pages 5, 17, and 19; Mary Ann Wilson gave hers for pages 21 and 39. Thank you both for giving me more than your hands! And for that, thank you to all of my family and friends too.

Milton Keynes UK
Ingram Content Group UK Ltd.
UKHW050642241123
433174UK00002B/8

9798985472806